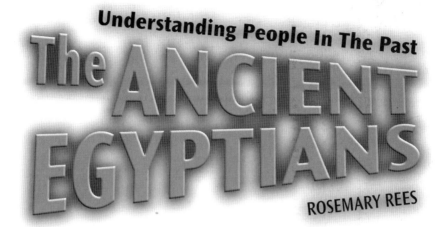

Understanding People In The Past
The ANCIENT EGYPTIANS

ROSEMARY REES

Heinemann
LIBRARY

www.heinemann.co.uk/library

Visit our website to find out more information about Heine

To order:

☎ Phone ++44 (0)1865 888066

📄 Send a fax to ++44 (0)1865 314091

💻 Visit the Heinemann Bookshop at www.heinemann.co.uk/libr and order online.

First published in Great Britain by Heinemann Library, Halley Court, Jordan Hill, Oxford OX2 8EJ, part of Harcourt Education.
Heinemann is a registered trademark of Harcourt Education Ltd.

Editorial: Clare Lewis and Katie Shepherd
Design: Michelle Lisseter and Damco Solutions Ltd
Picture research: Hannah Taylor
Production: Helen McCreath

Originated by Dot Gradations Ltd
Printed and bound in China by WKT Company Ltd

13-digit ISBN: 978 0 431 07792 5 (hb)
10 09 08 07 06
10 9 8 7 6 5 4 3 2 1

13-digit ISBN: 978 0 431 07805 2 (pb)
11 10 09 08 07
10 9 8 7 6 5 4 3 2 1

British Library Cataloging in Publication Data

Rees, Rosemary, 1942-
The Ancient Egyptians. - 2nd ed. - (Understanding People in the Past). 932'.01
A full catalogue record for this book is available from the British Library.

Acknowledgments

The author and publisher are grateful to the following for permission to reproduce copyright material:
By courtesy of the Trustees of the British Museum, pp. 23l, 31r, 33l, 36; C. M. Dixon, pp. 9, 21, 22, 24, 25r, 28r, 31l, 35, 37-39, 51l, 52, 54, 58; E. T. Archive, pp. 10, 12, 27a, 55, 56; Werner Forman Archive, pp. 8, 14, 26, 27b, 28l, 42l, 44, 48r, 49, 50, 53l; Michael Holford, pp. 5, 7, 13, 17l, 18, 20, 23r, 25l, 29, 34, 40l, 41, 43, 45, 46l, 48l, 51r, 54br, 57l, 59; Hutchison Library, pp. 6, 30, 40r, 46r; William Macquitty, pp. 11l, 17r, 33r, 42r; National Center for Supercomputing Applications, p. 11 r.

Cover photograph © Werner Forman Archive/Egyptian Musiem, Cairo

The publishers would like to thank Dr. Christina Riggs for her advice on the content of this book.

Every effort has been made to contact copyright holders of any material reproduced in this book. Any omissions will be rectified in subsequent printings if notice is given to the publisher.

Some words are shown in bold, **like this**. You can find out what they mean by looking in the glossary.

CONTENTS

WHO WERE THE EGYPTIANS?

About 5,000 years ago a new way of life grew up along the banks of the River Nile in Egypt. It lasted for more than 3,000 years. This is longer than any other **civilization** in the history of the world. Experts know more about the ancient Egyptians than they do about the ancient Greeks or Romans. This is because a great number of buildings and objects made by the ancient Egyptians can still be seen today.

A mixture of peoples
The people who settled in Egypt came from many different places. The red arrows on the map below show where they came from.

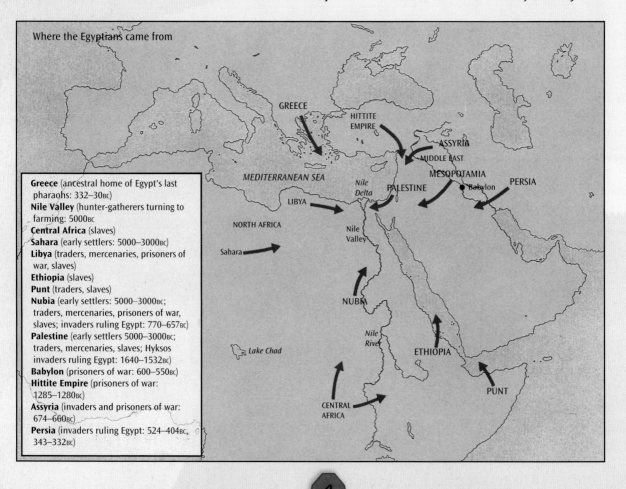

Where the Egyptians came from

GREECE

HITTITE EMPIRE

ASSYRIA

MIDDLE EAST

MESOPOTAMIA

PERSIA

MEDITERRANEAN SEA

Nile Delta

PALESTINE

Babylon

LIBYA

NORTH AFRICA

Nile Valley

Sahara

NUBIA

Nile River

Lake Chad

ETHIOPIA

PUNT

CENTRAL AFRICA

Greece (ancestral home of Egypt's last pharaohs: 332–30BC)
Nile Valley (hunter-gatherers turning to farming: 5000BC)
Central Africa (slaves)
Sahara (early settlers: 5000–3000BC)
Libya (traders, mercenaries, prisoners of war, slaves)
Ethiopia (slaves)
Punt (traders, slaves)
Nubia (early settlers: 5000–3000BC; traders, mercenaries, prisoners of war, slaves; invaders ruling Egypt: 770–657BC)
Palestine (early settlers 5000–3000BC; traders, mercenaries, slaves; Hyksos invaders ruling Egypt: 1640–1532BC)
Babylon (prisoners of war: 600–550BC)
Hittite Empire (prisoners of war: 1285–1280BC)
Assyria (invaders and prisoners of war: 674–660BC)
Persia (invaders ruling Egypt: 524–404BC, 343–332BC)

The early Egyptians

The very first people who lived by the River Nile lived mainly by hunting for meat and gathering wild plants. They kept some cows, sheep, and goats. They grew a few crops.

The Egyptians grew flax, barley, and a type of wheat called emmer. These plants did not grow wild in the Nile Valley. They had first been used by farmers in other parts of the Middle East. This means that some of the first Egyptian farmers probably came from these areas. However, the language, religion, and art that grew up in Egypt were very different from the rest of the Middle East. Many historians believe that most of the early farming people came from North Africa.

The Great Sphinx is guarding the stone pyramid you can see in the background. An Egyptian ruler, the **Pharaoh** *Khephren, was buried in the pyramid about 4,500 years ago. Egyptians dug the Great Sphinx out of the sand about 2,400 years ago. No one knows why the sphinx has the head of a man and the body of a lion.*

Dates from long ago

Almost all of the dates in this book are bc dates. They count the number of years *before* the birth of Jesus Christ. When dates are given for things that have happened *since* the birth of Christ, the letters ad come before the year. When historians are not sure about a date it is printed in this book with a question mark.

THE GIFT OF THE NILE

Seven thousand years ago the Nile Valley was mostly a swamp. Fewer than 30,000 people were able to live there, hunting animals and gathering crops. Land in other parts of the Middle East was far more fertile. Farmers in Mesopotamia grew a lot of food. They used dykes (ditches) and **irrigation** canals to control the flood water from their rivers. This made the soil rich and fertile. More and more people were able to live there because there was enough food for them.

This is the River Nile today. Only the land along the banks of the Nile is rich and fertile. Almost no rain falls in Egypt. The country still depends on the Nile for almost all of its water.

Egypt becomes fertile

Gradually the climate everywhere became drier. Less rain was falling in the African lands, far to the south, that fed water to the Nile. The level of the river fell. As it fell, a strip of rich, black land emerged along each of its banks. This was fertile soil. Every year the Nile flooded. Every year there was more rich, fertile soil. It was this soil that helped make Egypt such a great country. Eventually, 2,000 years ago, more than 2 million people lived and worked in the Nile Valley.

Egyptians painted these pictures on a scroll. They buried the scroll with an important official named Nakht. It shows what the Egyptians hoped for in life after death. They hoped for fertile fields surrounded by water.

The Black Land

"The Black Land" was the Egyptians' name for their country. This was because the fertile land along the Nile (shown in dark green) was black. On each side of the river were the "Red Lands". These were deserts. No one lived there. They protected the Black Lands from invasion by Egypt's enemies. So did the **cataracts** and rapids south of Egypt on the Nile.

Travel across the desert was difficult. This meant the Egyptians could not easily defend their **oases**. The Faiyum Oasis was the only one the Egyptians controlled all the time. This was because it was near the Nile and could be defended easily. The Egyptian pharaohs moved their troops by water up and down the Nile to meet their enemies who could only advance slowly across land.

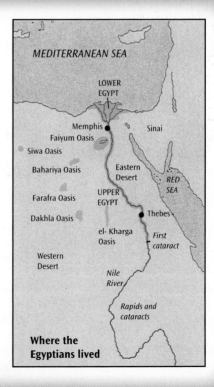

MEDITERRANEAN SEA

LOWER EGYPT

Memphis

Faiyum Oasis

Siwa Oasis

Bahariya Oasis

Farafra Oasis

Dakhla Oasis

Sinai

Eastern Desert

RED SEA

UPPER EGYPT

Thebes

el- Kharga Oasis

Western Desert

First cataract

Nile River

Rapids and cataracts

Where the Egyptians lived

HOW DO WE KNOW ABOUT THE EGYPTIANS?

About 300 people all over the world spend their time finding out about the Egyptians. They work in museums and universities. They are called Egyptologists.

Looking underneath the ground

Archaeologists are people who have been specially trained to **excavate** and uncover ruins of old buildings. They also find everyday objects (called artefacts) made by people in the past. From these they build up a picture of the past and how people lived.

Archaeologists have found homes on the edge of the desert that were lived in by ancient Egyptians. Remains of really ancient houses on the banks of the Nile have not been found, because they were swept away when the Nile flooded.

The tombs of important Egyptians have also been discovered. In the tombs was everything the Egyptians believed that the person needed in the afterlife.

This is a wooden statue from the tombs at Sakkara. It is probably a priest, and is definitely more than 4,400 years old. The wood has not rotted at all because Egypt's climate is so hot and dry. All that has gone is the paint that originally covered the statue. In wetter countries the statue would have rotted away.

Looking at stones and papers

Some Egyptian tombs are under the ground. Others, such as the pyramids, are above ground and can be seen clearly. Archaeologists had to find a way in. They had to hope that grave robbers had not been there before them, thousands of years ago. Many temples are also still standing. Their carvings and statues tell us about the pharaohs and about Egyptian beliefs. We also know about Egypt through thousands of **papyrus** letters and documents that have survived in Egypt's dry air.

The golden mask of Tutankhamen
Tutankhamen was an unimportant pharaoh whose burial chamber was not robbed before it could be studied. Archaeologists found wonderful treasures there. This shows that more important pharaohs must have been surrounded by even greater treasures.

We know about Egyptian learning through writings on papyrus scrolls. This is part of a papyrus scroll. It was written in about 650 BC. It is a copy of a much older scroll.

LOOKING AFTER EGYPT'S PAST

In AD 1954 archaeologists were working near the base of the Great Pyramid of Khufu at Giza in Egypt. They found a sealed room. When they opened the room the air inside escaped. That ancient air had been trapped inside for 4,600 years. The archaeologists wished they had been able to analyze the air. They might have been able to find out something more about ancient Egypt. In AD 1987 archaeologists tried to capture some ancient air from a room nearby that they thought was sealed in the same way. When they pumped the air out, however, it smelled stale. The sealed room had been damaged. The air was not ancient at all. This shows us how difficult it is to study ancient sites without losing or destroying some evidence from the past.

Scientific archaeology

In the past a lot of information was lost because people just took objects from sites and gave them to museums. Now archaeologists make very careful notes of where every find is discovered.

Wall paintings tell us a lot about the lives of ancient Egyptians. The problem is that old paint fades very quickly. Today, archaeologists take photographs of the paintings they discover. Before photography, the paintings were copied. Giovanni Belzoni copied this painting from a tomb wall in Thebes. Many of the actual wall paintings he copied have faded away. As well as copying paintings, he sent many treasures to

Moving a temple out of harm's way

This ancient temple at Abu Simbel is being moved. If it stayed where it was it would have been under water when a new dam was built. These workmen have cut stones and are now lifting them out very carefully.

Looking without disturbing

Scientists used X-rays and computers to make a three-dimensional image of this unknown Egyptian's head. If they had unwrapped the body (called a mummy) it would not have lasted long.

Archaeologists know that every clue is important in putting together the story of the past. One problem is that many ancient objects fade and crumble when they are exposed to the light and air. Scientists can now preserve objects that have been in the ground for a long time.

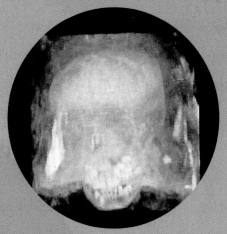

PICTURES AND PICTURE WRITING

When Egyptians painted pictures they were not trying to show what people really looked like. An Egyptian picture was like a diagram. Egyptians believed that their pictures had magical powers. For example, they made the picture painting on page 7 as a charm to help the dead nobleman's spirit feed itself in the afterlife.

Pictures with rules

This is part of a funeral stone. The artist has followed many rules in making the pictures and the writing. For example, the man is facing right. The woman is facing left. This means the man is more important than the woman. When two people face each other, the more important person always faces right.

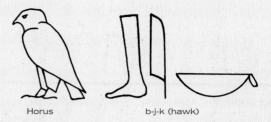

Horus   b-j-k (hawk)

Hieroglyphics

Egyptians sometimes wrote in pictures. This type of writing is called **hieroglyphics**. The Egyptians invented it about 5,000 years ago (around 3000 BC). They believed that hieroglyphs were magical. They used them mostly in temples and in tombs.

Spelling

All hieroglyphic symbols began as pictures. One picture stood for one whole word. This symbol of a hawk stood for the god Horus. Word pictures also worked as signs for sounds. These signs spelled the word "hawk".

Hieratic writing

There are thousands of pieces of everyday papyrus letters, official reports, and essays. They tell us that the Egyptians told jokes, complained, quarrelled, and sometimes behaved badly. Thieves robbed and judges took bribes; officials and generals plotted against their pharaohs; soldiers, peasants, and slaves ran away from their masters. These ordinary writings were in **hieratic script**, which did not use pictures and which could be written much more quickly than hieroglyphics. The Egyptians also used **demotic script**, which was a simple form of hieratic script. Demotic script was carved on the Rosetta Stone.

The Rosetta Stone
The same information was carved in hieroglyphics (top), demotic script (middle) and Greek (bottom). Jean Francois Champollion understood Greek and used it to work out the other languages.

THE PHARAOH KINGS OF EGYPT

The word pharaoh means "the one who lives in the palace". The Egyptian pharaoh kings had a long list of more official titles. The Egyptians believed that no single name could describe the greatness of their rulers. They gave the pharoahs names that compared them to the gods.

The royal dynasties

Egyptians believed that the queen had special connections to two goddesses. One goddess was Isis, the first goddess-queen of Egypt. The other was Hathor, the goddess of women, love, and happiness.

A line of rulers who pass on their throne from one member of their family to another over many, many years is called a **dynasty**. Sometimes dynasties died out. Sometimes they were overthrown by foreign conquerors. Over 3,000 years, 30 different dynasties ruled Egypt.

Before the first pharaohs, many kings fought for control of different parts of the Nile Valley. In this carving, King Narmer of **Upper Egypt** *is killing an enemy prisoner.*

Crown of Upper Egypt Crown of Lower Egypt Crown of All Egypt War crown Hemhemet crown

Crowns of the pharaohs
The pharoah kings of
Egypt wore these crowns
on different occasions.

The pharaohs of 3,000 years

Egyptologists try to work out when particular pharaohs ruled and when certain dynasties began and ended. They do this by studying the lists made by historians at the time of the ancient Egyptians. Some ancient scrolls mention comets and the position of stars. Modern **astronomy** can tell us when these comets and stars appeared in ancient times. Egyptologists can then work out more accurately when certain pharaohs ruled.

Egyptian dynasties are grouped by periods. The time before the pharaohs is called the **pre-dynastic period**. The time of the first pharaohs is called the **early period**. The most important periods, as far as the pharaohs were concerned, are called kingdoms.

Pre-dynastic period	5000–3100 BC (?)
Early dynastic period	3100–2649 BC (?)
Old Kingdom	2649–2134 BC (?)
Middle Kingdom	2040–1640 BC (?)
New Kingdom	1550–1070 BC (?)

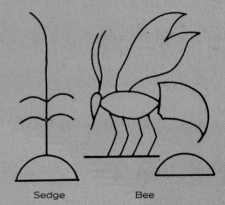

Sedge   Bee

Two words for king
A sedge (a type of plant) was the
Lower Egyptian *sign for royalty; a*
bee was the Upper Egyptian sign.
These are the hieroglyphs for them.

THE PHARAOHS AND THE GODS

The Egyptians spoke to their pharaoh (king) as if he was a god. In fact, they gave him five names, each one linked to a god or goddess. His name at birth was the "son of Ra". Ra was the Sun god and Egypt's chief god. Other names referred to Horus, the hawk god, and to Nakhbet and Wadjet, the goddesses who protected Upper and Lower **Egypt**.

When a pharaoh died, he also took on the name of the god Osiris. Osiris was the god of the **underworld**, the place where all good Egyptians went when they died.

This is the title of the Pharaoh Thotmes IV, written in hieroglyphics.

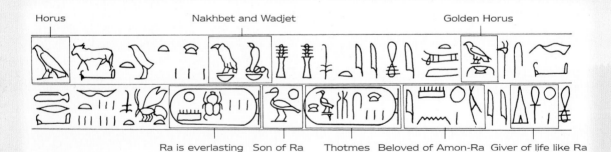

Horus   Nakhbet and Wadjet   Golden Horus

Ra is everlasting   Son of Ra   Thotmes   Beloved of Amon-Ra   Giver of life like Ra

The official title of the Pharoah Thotmes IV includes several god-like names. The pharaoh's last two names – Thotmes and "Ra is everlasting" – were the most important. They were written inside an oval loop of rope, known as a cartouche. The cartouche symbolizes the eternal circle of life, and it magically protects the words inside it.

The story of Osiris

Osiris was the god-king of Egypt. His brother Set cut Osiris' body into pieces. Set scattered the pieces up and down the Nile, so he could seize the country for himself. Isis found the pieces and put them back together. Osiris became king of the underworld. Horus, the son of Osiris and his wife Isis, fought with Set for the throne of Egypt. The gods approved of Horus and he became the rightful king. By calling their pharaoh "Horus" the Egyptians were saying that he was their rightful king.

Giver of life
This is a wall carving in a temple. The god Ra is giving an anhk to the pharaoh. An ankh is the hieroglyphic symbol for life.

Osiris, king of the underworld
In this picture a man who has died is giving gifts to the god, Osiris.

THE PYRAMID-BUILDERS

The Egyptians built pyramids to hold the tombs of their pharaohs. Archaeologists have so far discovered more than 60 pyramids. There may be more, lying under the desert sands.

Leading the world in stonework

Pyramids are the first buildings made by precisely cutting and putting together great blocks of stone. In this way, the Egyptians led the world in stonework for 2,000 years.

*The **step pyramid** looks like this today. The drawing below shows what it looked like when it was first built. It was the very first pyramid. It was built for the Pharaoh Zoser by his great scribe Imhotep.*

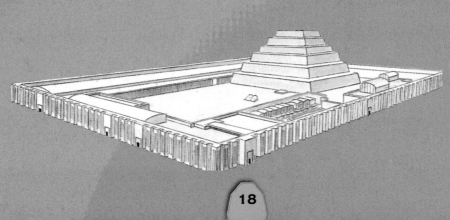

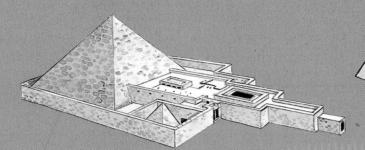

A **true pyramid** had smooth sides and came to a point. This is a drawing of the pyramid at Abusir. It was finished more than 4,400 years ago.

How were the pyramids built?
The work gangs probably built huge ramps of sand and used rollers to haul the great stones up the ramps.

Why the pyramids were built

Before the pyramids, Egyptians buried their pharaohs in **mastabas**. These were long, low buildings made from bricks or small stones.

Zoser (2630–2611 BC) was one of the first pharaohs of the **Old Kingdom**. When he died the Egyptians decided to put his body in a pyramid. They decided that this pyramid should rise by steps so that Zoser's spirit could climb to meet the sun. Later, the Egyptians built pyramids with smooth sides. The Egyptians built most of their pyramids near Memphis, which was the capital of ancient Egypt. It is not far from Cairo, the modern capital.

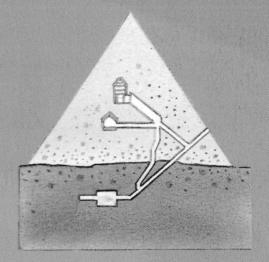

Inside a pyramid
Pyramids were mostly filled with stones and rubble. There were also passageways leading to the burial chamber of the pharaoh. Sometimes the Egyptians built false chambers and passageways that led nowhere. This was to confuse grave robbers.

DEATH AND LIFE AFTER DEATH

Egyptians believed that, at the end of every day, the Sun god Ra died in the western sky at sunset. Everyone in Egypt prayed for his return. Ra was reborn every morning at sunrise.

The Egyptians thought that, when Ra died each evening, he went down into the underworld. This was a perfect place, which brought Ra back to life as he journeyed through it. The Egyptians believed that they, too, could reach this world if their bodies were preserved when they died.

The judgment of the gods
The god of mummification, Anubis, is weighing a dead man's heart. The heart is on one side of the scale; a feather, representing truth, is on the other. If the scales did not balance, monsters would come and eat the dead man's soul.

Funeral ceremonies
In this picture four priests are opening the mummy's mouth with a specially shaped stick. This is so that he can eat in the afterlife.

Making a home for a spirit

The Egyptians made a dead person's body into a mummy that would never decay. They believed that this gave a lasting home to the person's **ka**, or body-spirit. The person's soul, or **ba**, could move through the underworld and return to Earth as long as the ka survived.

The Egyptians mummified their pharaohs and put them in unchanging tombs of stone – the pyramids. Wealthy Egyptians made their own arrangements to be mummified. People who were too poor to afford this hoped that their ba would join the "boat of millions". This was a golden ship full of good souls in which Ra crossed and re-crossed the sky.

A tombstone inscription
Most Egyptian tombstones were like this one. It reminded the living that they should make offerings to Osiris, the god of the underworld. They should do this on behalf of the dead.

Hathor, goddess of women and trees
Hathor is pouring water to quench the thirst of a dead woman's ka and ba.

MUMMIES AND MEDICINES

The Egyptians thought that the dead needed their bodies as much as the living did. A person's soul needed somewhere to live after death. This is why they preserved people's bodies when they died.

Making a mummy

Caring for bodies was the work of priests. The priests made a dead body into a mummy. They learned, by making mummies, how bodies work.

Making a mummy naturally
This Egyptian died about 5,000 years ago. The desert sand dried and preserved his body. The clay pots were there because the Egyptians thought he might need them in his next life.

Visiting the doctor

Most priests were also doctors. They prescribed medicines. Some of the medicines were made from herbs. Treatments for illnesses could involve **sacrifices** to the gods, spells, and wearing charms. Some priest-doctors set bones skilfully, and bandaged wounds.

Egyptian ideas spread to Greece

In the winter of 332–331 BC, Alexander the Great conquered Egypt. Egypt became part of the Greek Empire. Alexander set up a new city, Alexandria. Here the Greeks started a university and a library. They gathered together all the knowledge they could find from Egypt. Egyptian knowledge and understanding about **anatomy** and disease spread all over the Greek Empire.

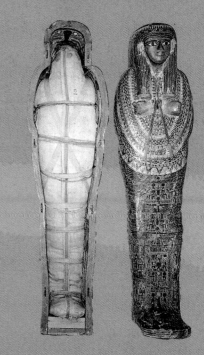

Making mummies
This mummy is a priestess from Thebes. She died in about 1000 BC. When she died, priests covered her body in natron. This is a chemical made from salt. The natron drew water out of the body and so dried it. Then priests wrapped the mummy in linen bandages.

Canopic jars
Priests put a person's liver, intestines, stomach, and lungs into these special jars.

TEMPLES AND THEIR GODS

Egyptians worshipped more than 2,000 gods. Most of them were local spirits who controlled a particular hill or tree. At that place people built a small **shrine** out of mud bricks or matting. They put a clay model of the spirit inside. This was the home on Earth of the spirit. People prayed at the shrine and asked for favours. A few great gods were worshipped all over Egypt. Their images, made by the very best craftsworkers, were housed in golden shrines kept in stone temples.

Priests

Priests had to be very clean for the gods they served. Some of them shaved all the hair from their bodies. Others bathed in sacred pools. Ordinary priests could only do basic jobs like sweeping out the temple.

In the inner sanctuary of a temple was a golden shrine. Inside the shrine was a beautiful statue. The god of the temple was supposed to live in the statue. Every morning the senior priests broke the clay seal on the sanctuary door and brought the god out for worship.

Amon-Ra
This is a statue of the Sun god in the shape of Amon. The statue is almost 3,000 years old. It is made of solid silver and covered with gold.

The ruins of the temple of Amon at Karnak, near Thebes
These columns once supported the roof. The columns are so huge that 100 people could stand on the top of one of them. This temple was extremely rich. It had magnificent buildings and many full-time priests.

Priestesses

Only a few women became priestesses. However, the high-priestess of Amon was the most holy person in the entire area around Thebes, except for the pharaoh.

Gods of the pharaohs

The pharaohs could join the names of similar gods into one. This made the god even more powerful. For example, the Sun god Ra could be called Ra-Harakhty or Amon-Ra.

Animal-headed gods
Some gods had the heads of animals. The Egyptians believed that some animals were closely connected to magical powers. Animals, especially cats, were worshipped in many temples.

HOW WAS EGYPT GOVERNED?

The pharaoh of Egypt was an **absolute ruler**. He did not have to obey any laws himself. He could change any laws he wanted. However, to be a good ruler, a pharaoh needed help from other people. He would have had a very difficult time if important people such as priests, generals, and landowners thought that he was offending the gods. They might think this if he changed too many laws or did not look after the needs of Egypt.

The pharaoh had to let other people decide some things for him. He could not be everywhere, or make all the decisions. Most of his decisions were made by the scribes.

Scribes, generals, and priests

The younger sons of landowners and nobles trained to be scribes. The wealthiest of them went to the great school for scribes at Thebes. They learned history, poetry, surveying, architecture, and accountancy. Most of them went into the pharaoh's service as government officials.

Scribes
Scribes like this ran Egypt. They worked in mud-brick offices in small villages along the banks of the River Nile. They collected taxes, settled legal arguments, worked as priests, designed and organized the construction of public buildings, and persuaded young men to join the army in times of war.

Taxes

This magical figure was buried with a rich man. Making a tomb and buying tomb equipment, such as this figure, were very expensive, and every item was taxed as well. There was even a tax for burying the dead person.

The pharaoh's closest advisers were scribes belonging to Egypt's most important families. One scribe, the **vizier**, became the pharaoh's prime minister.

Women scribes

Very few women learned to read and write in ancient Egypt. However, the Egyptians had a feminine word for scribe, so we know that some scribes must have been women. However, we know very little about them.

Women rulers

Egypt was ruled at least three times by women:

Nefrusobk	1787–1783 BC
Hatshepsut	1473–1458 BC (?)
Twosre	1198–1196 BC (?)

Nefertiti, the great royal queen of the Pharaoh Akhnaton, took a very active part in his reign (1353–1335 BC (?)).

During the **Greek period** (332–30 BC) Greek-speaking queens such as Arsinoe, Berenice, and Cleopatra ruled Egypt. They did this either by themselves or with their husbands.

Cleopatra VII, the last Greek-speaking queen

WHAT DID THE EGYPTIANS WEAR?

Egypt is a hot country, although winter nights can be very cold. People wore clothes to keep them cool or warm, and to protect them from the Sun. The clothes people wore showed their position in society.

Men's clothes

Men usually wore a skirt, or kilt. A peasant's kilt was made from coarse fabric and was tucked up to keep his legs free when he worked in the fields. A noble's kilt was long and made from fine linen.

An important official and his wife
Their clothes are made from fine linen. The man's necklace and braided hair show that he has an important job. This statue was made from limestone in about 2550 BC.

Children
Most children wore no clothes at all. These boys came from a rich family. You can tell this because their hair has been carefully tied into side locks. Servants would have done this for them. Very young children had their heads shaved.

Women's clothes

Peasant women wore dresses made from coarse fabric. Wealthy women wore dresses made from fine linen. They were usually bleached white, but some were dyed orange, yellow, or green. The best dresses were pleated.

Make-up and hairstyles

Men and women wore green or black eye make-up, especially on special occasions.

Rich women either wore their hair long, or cut it off and wore wigs. Rich men could also wear wigs. Peasants and farmers kept their hair short.

Fine clothes
This man and his wife are wearing linen dresses. The cloth is so finely woven that you can see through it. The woman has a cone of animal fat on top of her head. It melts slowly into her hair and makes it smell nice.

Glazed ceramic jewellery
This jewellery was made 2,500 years ago. It was everyday jewellery for rich people. Peasant women wore beads, but their beads were crudely made. On special occasions rich people wore lotus flowers, gold rings, earrings, necklaces, bracelets, and anklets.

AN EGYPTIAN VILLAGE

Most Egyptians in ancient times lived in villages. The only towns were Memphis and Thebes. The Egyptians built their villages on the banks of canals or rivers. They used boats when they needed to travel to another village.

Many people were in the fields looking after crops and animals. Craftsworkers would stay in the village, making pots, preparing food, or building things. Village women worked as weavers. From a very young age, children helped their parents at work.

A modern Egyptian village near Luxor
This modern village looks very much like an ancient one. Ancient Egyptian villages were just a cluster of flat-topped houses built from mud bricks. The houses were built along narrow streets leading from the marketplace. Most houses had two or three rooms.

The village market

Market days were always very busy occasions. People came from the villages up and down the river. Local craftsworkers and peasant women laid out goods to sell on cloths that they spread on the ground. There was food and drink for sale: salt, barley, onions, peas, beans, barley bread, and beer. People liked to buy fresh, salted, or dried fish from the River Nile. Craftspeople sold what they had made. This could be, for example, woven wicker baskets, leather, jewellery, or clay pots. Magicians would also be there, selling medical advice and magic charms to protect the villagers from evil.

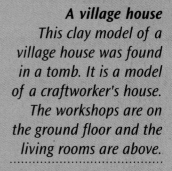

People used donkeys to carry anything heavy. Dogs and pigs nosed around trying to find tasty bits of food that had been thrown out.

Landowners and senior scribes had large homes on the edges of villages. Their homes were surrounded by high walls. Sometimes very important people had houses that stood apart from the villages.

A village house
This clay model of a village house was found in a tomb. It is a model of a craftworker's house. The workshops are on the ground floor and the living rooms are above.

A village market scene
The villagers are going to be able to buy some fresh beef.

WHAT WERE THE EGYPTIANS' HOMES LIKE?

Archaeologists have not been able to excavate many Egyptian homes. This is because the floodwaters of the Nile swept most of them away. However, in the desert near the royal tombs, the ancient Egyptians built some special villages. These were for workers and craftspeople to live in while they worked on the tombs.

A craftsperson's house

The desert houses were built side by side along a street. The houses were long and narrow, as you can see from the drawing below.

Inside a craftsperson's home
This is a modern drawing of the inside of a craftsperson's house. It was built 3,500 years ago at Deir el-Medina near Thebes.

Roof Fence

Door to bedroom

Palm logs and thatch

Workroom

Mud-brick oven

Open-air kitchen

Vent

Cellar

Cellar

Birth shrine

Pillar

Shrine

Part of the front room was bricked off to make a shrine. Here the family left food for their ancestors. Babies were born here. The parents hoped that the ancestors would make sure that no wicked souls were born into the family. The next room was the main one in the house. Small windows high in the wall let in light. There were mud benches around the walls. In the walls there were shrines to gods. Two narrow rooms came next. One was a bedroom with sleeping mats on the floor. The other was a room where the craftspeople worked. Steps at the back led up to the roof. The family ate their evening meal and sometimes slept on the roof. The kitchen was also outdoors, in a small courtyard at the back of the house.

Bes, god of the household
Every home had a shrine with the image of Bes in it. He was the god of women, children, and childbirth.

Bedroom furniture
The Egyptians stretched canvas across the bed frame and slept on it. Instead of a pillow they used a headrest, which you can see on the floor at the back of the frame.

FAMILY LIFE

Most of what we know about Egyptian life has been told to us by Egyptian men. They were mainly interested in what men did. They do give us glimpses, however, of what life was like for women and children.

Husbands and wives

Powerful men, such as the pharaoh, had more than one wife. Most men had only one.

Nebamon and his family
This is a painting from Nebamon's tomb. It shows him hunting birds in the marshes. Can you see his wife and daughter? Egyptians painted the people they thought were less important smaller than important people.

Egyptian women were allowed to own property. Most women living in other countries at the same time could not do this. Archaeologists found a scroll written in 1156 BC by the tax assessor for the Faiyum Oasis. It shows that about 10 per cent of the land belonged to women. Women also owned the furniture in their homes.

Children

When children were young, they played games and sports, and they helped their parents at home or in the fields. In ordinary families, children did not go to school. In wealthy families, young boys learned to read and write at the temple school.

Cats

Egyptians thought that cats were sacred. They believed that male cats represented the Sun, and female cats the goddess Bast. All cats were supposed to be looked after by Sekhmet, the fierce goddess of war. Whole temples were devoted to cat worship. It was forbidden to take cats out of Egypt. Special commissioners were sent to other countries to buy back cats that had been smuggled away.

This mummy of a cat was made about 3,000 years ago.

HUNTING AND BOATING, FEASTS AND FUN

All Egyptians enjoyed themselves. They had plenty of fun in their free time. Most of what we know about their free time comes from tomb paintings of rich people.

Children

Children played tug of war and leapfrog. Egyptian children had wooden toys, dolls, slings, and balls for games.

Feasts

Rich people held banquets. Servants offered wine and dishes of delicious food to the guests. Everyone ate with their fingers. They rinsed their fingers in dishes of perfumed water which the servants brought around later.

A horse on wheels
This was a child's toy. Other toys were carved monkeys and wooden dolls. There were wooden cats, leopards, and mice with mouths that opened and closed when children pulled a string.

Playing senet
An Egyptian noble called Ani and his wife are playing a game called senet. The rules have been lost, but archaeologists have found many senet boards and pieces. This picture was painted over 3,200 years ago.

Hunting and boating

Wealthy families could sail their boats on the Nile. Sometimes, wealthy men are shown hunting birds or going fishing. Very rich people also had horses and chariots.

Dancing girls and musicians
Musicians were often women. As well as hand-clapping and flute playing, the women played harps, lutes, and finger drums. We know what the instruments sounded like, because they have survived. We do not know what music they played, because no music was ever written down.

COOKING AND EATING

Food for the poor

Egyptian peasants mainly ate barley bread and onions. They made barley flour into porridge. They drank a lot of beer. Sometimes they ate fish, and, from time to time, garlic, green vegetables, dates, figs, chickpeas, and lentils. Not many Egyptians ever tasted the types of food eaten by the rich.

Food for the rich

The rich had more than 40 different types of bread to choose from. They were fond of roasted quails, pigeon stew, kidneys, beef ribs, fresh berries, barley cakes, and cheese. They ate chicken, salted goose, and wild game from the Nile marshes. They also got luxury vegetables from the marshes: wild celery, papyrus stalks, and lotus root. Fishermen caught eels, mullet, carp, giant perch, and tigerfish in the Nile and in the canals.

The Egyptians sometimes left cooked meals in tombs. These were for the souls of the dead. Archaeological remains of these meals, as well as tomb paintings, tell us a lot about cooking and eating.

A servant fans a charcoal cooking fire
The Egyptians did their cooking in outdoor kitchens. Kitchens were kept cool by a roof of reed matting or thatch made of palm leaves.

The Egyptians grew grapes and made wine from them. Wine was only for the rich people.

Making beer 4,400 years ago
The Egyptians first mashed barley bread into a pot of water. Then they added some old beer with live yeast in it. They let the mixture stand for about a week. Then they strained out the bread and drank the liquid quickly. If they left it, the beer would soon turn into vinegar.

Grinding barley
The model above was made 4,000 years ago. The woman is pushing a small stone backwards and forwards over a stone slab piled with cracked barley. She is grinding the barley into flour.

THE FARMING YEAR

The Egyptians had three seasons. Each season lasted for four months. The first season was the time of the flood, called **akhet**. It lasted from August to October. Then came **peret**, the time of planting and fresh growth. From March to August was the dry season, called **shemu**, when the crops ripened and were harvested.

The season of the flood

No farming could be done while the Nile flooded. Peasants travelled to temples, shrines, and markets. Villages held festivals to honour local spirits. The pharaoh's scribes ordered landowners to send peasants to work on public projects such as building pyramids or temples.

The shadoof
This is a shadoof being used in Egypt today. The shadoof was used 4,000 years ago. Water for crops is lifted out of the river in a goatskin bag, which swings around onto the bank to be emptied.

Harvesting grain
Egyptians are cutting the grain with sickles. These were made of curved pieces of wood with sharp flints stuck into them. The men are taking the cut grain to the threshing floor. There, oxen will walk over the stalks and separate them from the ears of grain.

Winnowing
After the threshing, peasants throw the grain in the air. The chaff (the light outer covering) blows away. The grains fall to the ground. Other peasants collect the grain and store it in granaries.

Sowing and reaping

The busiest time of the farming year came just after the flood. Men with wooden hoes, and cattle pulling wooden ploughs, turned over the new soil left by the flood. They dug it into the fields. Peasants scattered the seeds for new crops. Then they drove a herd of cows, goats, or pigs over the field. Their hooves pressed the seeds firmly into the ground.

Then the peasants could do other jobs. They repaired any damage done by the floods, they weeded, and they watered the crops.

Everyone helped at harvest time. Men, women, and children worked hard. They had to finish the harvest before the flood waters covered the fields once again.

CRAFTS AND CRAFTSWORKERS

Five thousand years ago, Egyptian craftsworkers produced wonderful objects in stone, copper, gold, and wood. We know this because archaeologists have found these objects in the tombs of the pharaohs. Almost all of the objects were made in the same style for thousands of years. It takes a real expert to tell whether something was made 4,500, 3,500, or 2,500 years ago.

Before the pharaohs

Egyptian **hunter-gatherers** produced the finest arrowheads and stone tools anywhere in the world. When they settled down and began farming, they made pottery and leather goods, and wove beautiful baskets.

Raised relief
This was a special type of sculpture. Artists cut away all the stone in the background around the figures. The figures were then carved so that they stood out from the stone. Raised relief was usually used inside temples. In this scene, a pharaoh is making offerings to the Sun god Ra.

Sunken relief
These figures are cut into the stone. The Egyptians usually used sunken relief outdoors, because it showed up better in sunshine.

Craftsworkers at the time of the pharaohs

Craftsworkers made painted stone statues and reliefs for temples and pyramids. They worked in groups. A senior scribe drew a plan on papyrus. It was marked on a squared grid to make copying easier. The stone or plaster was marked with the same grid, and the plan was copied on to it. Statues and reliefs were always painted, although today most of the paint has worn away. Artists who painted the sculptures followed a plan on a grid, just like the sculptors did.

The metalworker's art
In very early times, the Egyptians made beautiful things from copper. They made these jugs, bowls, and pots from about 2300 BC.

TRADE AND TRADE ROUTES

Each Egyptian village produced all that the villagers needed to live. They produced barley, onions, lentils, and bread to eat, cloth for clothes, mud bricks for building, and clay pots for storage. They traded with other villages and foreigners to get more variety and better quality goods.

Trade between Egyptians

The Egyptians did not use money. Instead, they took something with them to market to swap for the goods they wanted to buy. This is called barter. For example, a skilled craftsperson might barter a carved walking stick for a sack of wheat.

The Queen of Punt
The large lady in this relief is the Queen of Punt. She had a disease that made her legs and arms swell. The rest of the relief shows a procession of men carrying gifts from the Queen of Punt to Queen Hatshepsut of Egypt. Queen Hatshepsut sent an expedition into Punt to trade for frankincense, which was used in temple rituals.

Salt was important to the Egyptians. It was sold in most village markets. Salt came from the Nile **Delta**, where sea water was left in lagoons to evaporate. Traders took the salt by boat up the Nile to village markets. Some villages specialized in luxury goods. The best pots, for example, were made in the village with the best clay. For special linen, beer, or bread, Egyptians had to spend an hour or two travelling on the river.

Herbs from the land of Punt
In this relief, Queen Hatshepsut's soldiers are carrying herbs from the land of Punt. The Egyptians traded a lot of African goods, such as frankincense, with Mediterranean countries.

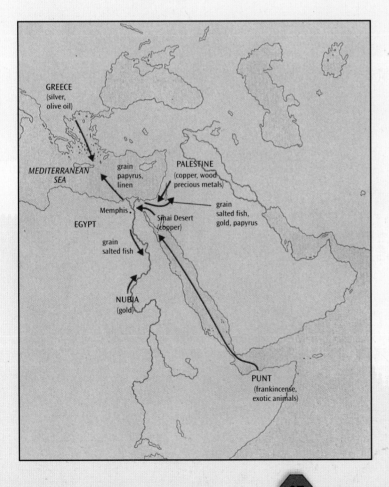

GREECE
(silver, olive oil)

MEDITERRANEAN
SEA

grain
papyrus,
linen

PALESTINE
(copper, wood
precious metals)

Memphis

Sinai Desert
(copper)

grain
salted fish,
gold, papyrus

EGYPT

grain
salted fish

NUBIA
(gold)

PUNT
(frankincense,
exotic animals)

Trade with other countries
Egypt had grain, salted fish, ropes, and papyrus scrolls, which other countries needed. Egypt also had gold, which other countries wanted. Egyptian traders bartered these goods for things not found in the Nile Valley. They bartered them for wood, copper, silver, and olive oil.

TRAVEL AND TRANSPORT

The Egyptians could not use carts and wagons to carry goods and people long distances. This was because the wheels would just sink into the sand. They used rollers to move vast blocks of stone across the desert when they were building the pyramids, but no wagons. In 1550 BC Egyptians built the very first Egyptian vehicle with wheels. This was a war chariot.

Egyptians carried goods and people around their country by using the River Nile. They also used donkeys to carry loads to remote oases. Later they used camels. However, one boat could carry a lot more than one pack animal, and Egyptians only used animals when they had to.

A donkey
Ancient Egyptians used donkeys for short, local journeys and for carrying burdens across the desert. The first donkeys they used were not big enough for riders.

River transport
Ancient Egyptians used the Nile to carry people and goods long distances. This boat (from about 400 BC) uses oars and sails to make it go faster.
The hieroglyph for "travelling south" was a boat with sails, because winds in Egypt blow from the north. The sign for "travelling north" was a boat with oars.

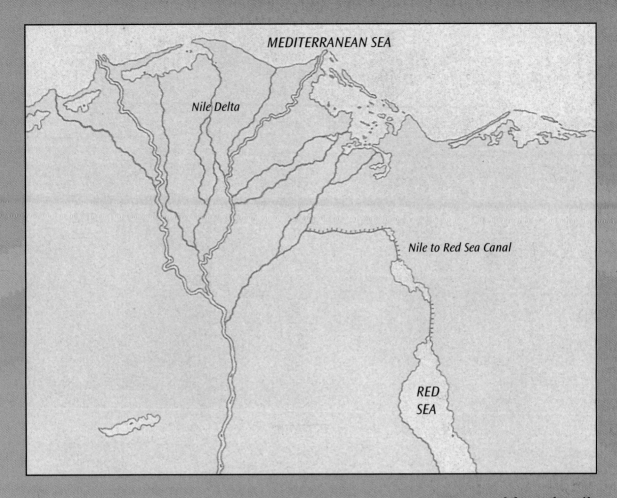

MEDITERRANEAN SEA

Nile Delta

Nile to Red Sea Canal

RED
SEA

The Nile waterway

The Egyptians managed very well without wheels or camels because they had the great River Nile. The Nile carried almost everything and everyone needing to travel.

In the days before the pharaohs, Egyptians made all their boats from papyrus reeds. Later, wood from Palestine made it possible for them to build better boats. Egyptians sailed these wooden boats to Palestine, through the Red Sea and down the east coast of Africa. Fishermen and peasants continued to use small papyrus boats on local trips.

A canal from the Nile to the Red Sea
This canal was finished in 490 BC. It was about 85 kilometres (53 miles) long. It made trading expeditions to Africa and Arabia easier for the Egyptians.

THE OLD KINGDOM

The Egyptians began to write down their own history in about 3100 BC. At about the same time, the Pharaoh Menes united the kingdoms of the Nile Valley and the Nile Delta to make Egypt one country. He named Memphis in the north and Abydos in the south as his capital cities.

The Great Pyramid of Khufu

Average weight of each block	2.5 tonnes
Total number of blocks	2.3 million
Years of Pharaoh Khufu's reign	23
Blocks set each year	100,000
Blocks set each day	285

The royal god, Horus the hawk
This is a statue of Pharaoh Khephren (2520–2492 BC). The god Horus the hawk is sitting by his shoulder. This tells the Egyptians that Khephren had the god's permission to rule.

The pyramids at Giza
These pyramids are the greatest in the history of Egypt. The largest is the Great Pyramid of Khufu (2551–2528 BC). Khufu taxed the Egyptian people very heavily so that he had enough money to build his pyramid.

The Old Kingdom lasted for about 500 years from 2649 BC to 2134 BC. The first pharaohs of the Old Kingdom did great things.

Pharaoh Zoser (2630–2611(?) BC)

Ancient Egyptians built the first ever pyramid for this pharaoh. Modern Egyptians look back to the reign of Pharaoh Zoser and call it a golden age. It was a time when learning and wisdom were very important. The pharaoh's scribe, Imhotep, was a powerful man. He helped develop architecture, sculpture, and medicine in Egypt.

Pharaoh Snofru (2575–2552(?) BC)

Snofru conquered part of northern Nubia. He built a lot of temples and three small pyramids. It was during his reign that worship of the Sun god Ra became especially important.

The collapse of the Old Kingdom

Gradually the pharaohs lost a lot of their power. Local governors, the **nomarchs**, ruled independently. It was as though Egypt was ruled by many kings.

Pharaoh Zoser
This statue of Zoser has a battered face. Thieves damaged it thousands of years ago when they stole the jewels that were set into the eye sockets.

THE MIDDLE KINGDOM

The Pharaoh Mentuhotpe fought many battles and finally united Egypt. He called himself "Uniter of the Two Lands" and said he was a god. People who study Egyptian history say that it was during his reign, from about 2040 BC, that a new age began.

The next Mentuhotpe pharaohs

The next two pharaohs were also called Mentuhotpe. They ruled Egypt from Thebes. They opened up the Red Sea trade route and Egypt became more prosperous. Temple building began again, and the pharaohs ordered new quarries to be opened. Amon, the god of the people who lived in Thebes, became very important.

Amenhemhet I (1991–1962 BC)

Amenhemhet started off as the vizier (prime minister) of the last Mentuhotpe pharaoh. He became a pharaoh, and built a new capital city, Itjtawy, near Memphis.

Senwosret I (1971–1926 BC)

At first, Senwosret ruled jointly with his father, Amenhemhet. They ordered many fine stone buildings to be built.

This relief shows Senwosret I with the god Ptah.

Senwosret III (1878–1841(?) BC)

Senwosret III was the greatest pharaoh of the **Middle Kingdom**. He kept a full-time army. His soldiers fought in Nubia and Palestine. Egypt became very powerful, and the pharaoh's government became stronger than ever before.

Queen Nefrusobk (1787–1783(?) BC)

When Senwosret III died, his officials kept the country peaceful. Gradually, however, they took more and more power for themselves. At this time Egypt had its first woman pharaoh, Queen Nefrusobk. We know almost nothing about her. Why do you think this is?

Senwosret III (1878–1841(?) BC)
This statue of Senwosret III shows him as a worried older man.

Amenhemhet III (1844–1797(?) BC)
This picture shows him destroying his enemies. In fact, his long reign was a time of peace.

THE NEW KINGDOM

In the 15th century BC the Egyptian pharaohs, who ruled from Thebes, began a struggle to expel the **Hyksos** pharaohs from Egypt. The Hyksos pharaohs were descended from immigrants, who had moved into Egypt from Palestine. They ruled the Nile Delta.

The Hyskos used bronze and iron. They fought in horse-drawn chariots. Their weapons were well designed. If the Egyptians wanted to defeat them, they had to learn a whole new technology quickly. This is just what happened. The Egyptians made chariots and weapons with the new metals. They learned to use horses. After many battles against the Hyskos, the Egyptians finally won. They ended up in charge of an united Egypt.

Amenhotep I (1525–1504(?) BC)
This pharaoh extended the Egyptian empire south into Nubia.

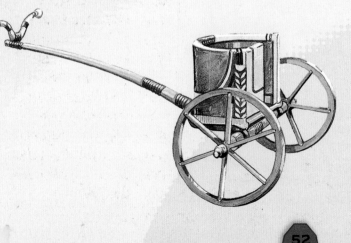

A horse-drawn war chariot
*The **New Kingdom** began when the Egyptians from Thebes defeated the Hyksos in the Nile Delta.*

Thotmes I (1504–1492(?) BC)

Thotmes I conquered Nubia, Syria, and Palestine and kept them under Egyptian rule. Egypt grew strong and powerful.

Hatshepsut (1473–1458(?) BC)

Hatshepsut was a powerful queen. When her husband, Thotmes II, died, the next person to be pharaoh was only a child. Hatshepsut ruled as **regent** for her nephew, Thotmes III. After seven years she said she was king. Thotmes III did not take charge until Hatshepsut was dead.

The next three pharaohs kept the empire strong. They gave a lot of money for temple building and to the gods to thank them for the victories that made Egypt united.

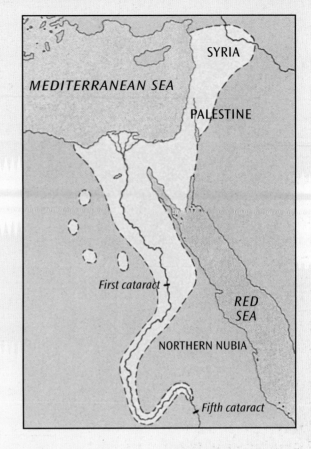

SYRIA

MEDITERRANEAN SEA

PALESTINE

First cataract

RED SEA

NORTHERN NUBIA

Fifth cataract

The Egyptian Empire
This map shows the Egyptian Empire when it was at its largest. The pharaoh was Thotmes I.

The funerary temple of Queen Hatshepsut
This was looked after by priests after the death of the queen. They made offerings to the gods on her behalf. Many years after her death, some of Hatshepsut's statues were destroyed, but other parts of her temple were still used.

AKHNATON

The Pharaoh Amenhotep IV inherited the throne of Egypt in around 1353 BC. His wife was Queen Nefertiti. Amenhotep and Nefertiti started a new religion in Egypt. This new religion was the worship of the sun god, Aton. Because of this he changed his name to Akhnaton.

The new religion

Akhnaton wanted the Egyptians to worship only Aton. He closed the temples of all the other gods. This made their priests very angry. Akhnaton built a new capital, Akhtaton, half way between Memphis and Thebes. At its centre was a temple without a roof, open to the Sun.

Queen Nefertiti
This is a sculpture of Queen Nefertiti. She was very beautiful. She was clever, too, and influenced Akhnaton's decisions. Below is a relief carving of Akhnaton.

Painting and sculpture

During the reign of Akhnaton, a new and different type of art began. Artists and sculptors began showing people in a more relaxed way. They drew people with round stomachs and thighs, with long necks and heads. This was considered beautiful. King Akhnaton and his family were still shown as more important than everyone else.

Akhnaton, Nefertiti, and their daughters
This relief carving was made to show the Pharaoh's love for his wife and daughters. Behind them are rays of sunlight. Each ray is giving an ankh, the symbol of life, to the royal family.

THE LAST DAYS OF EMPIRE

Egypt's enemies got stronger during Akhnaton's rule. Many people thought this happened because the old gods were angry. The nobles and the army remembered that when they worshiped Amon instead of Aton, they always had victories.

Tutankhamen

Tutankhamen became pharaoh after Akhnaton. He was just a boy when his rule began. His guardians moved the capital to Thebes. They changed his name from Tutankhatun to Tutankhamen to honour the old god, Amon. In these ways they hoped their luck would change, and Egypt would become powerful again.

Ramses II (1290–1224(?) BC)

During the time of Akhnaton, the Hittites took over Syria. Now, 50 years later, Ramses II fought them to a standstill in southern Syria. He made a peace with them that lasted for 50 years. He married several Hittite princesses to show he was friendly towards the Hittites.

The pharaoh Tutankhamen
Tutankhamen died when he was young. He is remembered because of the wonderful riches left in his tomb. They were never taken by robbers. We can see them in the Egyptian museum in Cairo today.

The pharaohs lose power

Egypt gradually lost control of more and more land outside Egypt. They lost Palestine, Nubia, and Syria. Inside Egypt, the priests became more and more powerful. Before long they were more powerful than the pharaohs. The temples bought more and more land and property. We know this by looking at the tax that was paid, and at who paid it. In the end, the priests of Thebes ruled Upper Egypt without the pharaohs. The pharaohs controlled only the Nile Delta.

Seti I
(1305–1290(?) BC)
Seti ordered Akhnaton's name to be taken off temple walls. He fought battles in Syria with his son, Ramses II.

Ramses II
(1290–1224(?) BC)
Ramses II built more temples and more enormous statues of himself than any other pharaoh in history. He had hundreds of wives, and more than 100 children. Egypt became poorer during his reign of 66 years.

FOREIGN RULE

Slowly, other countries in the Middle East and the Mediterranean grew stronger. Their soldiers had iron weapons, and their farmers had iron tools. They used camels to move goods and people.

The Greeks

Alexander the Great conquered Egypt in 332 BC. Egypt became part of the Greek Empire. For over 300 years Greek-speaking pharaohs, including Queen Cleopatra, ruled Egypt. Their capital city was Alexandria in Lower Egypt. Alexandria became a world centre of Greek art, architecture, and thought.

Cleopatra and her son, Caesarion
This relief carving is on a wall of the temple of Hathor in Dendera. Cleopatra and Caesarion ruled jointly over Egypt. Here they are making offerings to the Egyptian goddess, Hathor.

A mixture of cultures
This is an Egyptian mummy case. The painting on the front is a Roman painting. It is of a young Roman named Artemidorus who came from a rich Greek-Egyptian family. He died around ad 100, at about 20 years of age.

The Romans

The Romans took control of Egypt in 30 BC. More and more, the Egyptians used Greek and Roman ways of doing things, even in art. After AD 300, the Egyptians became Christians like the rest of the Roman Empire. In AD 640, the Arab people conquered Egypt and introduced their religion, Islam.

TIMELINE

BC

5000–3100?	Pre-dynastic period. Egyptians stop being hunter-gatherers and become farmers. Craftworkers use stone, copper, clay, wood, and leather. Egyptians trade with each other using papyrus boats.
3100	Menes becomes first pharaoh of all Egypt. Hieroglyphic writing begins to record Egyptian history.
3100–2649?	Capital at Memphis. Trade with Palestine and Nubia.
2649?	Beginning of the Old Kingdom.
2630–2611?	Reign of Zoser. Building of the step pyramid.
2575–2465?	The age of the true pyramids. Conquest of northern Nubia.
2134?	End of the Old Kingdom. Egypt breaks up into different parts.
2040?	Mentuhotpe brings different parts of Egypt together. Capital at Thebes. Beginning of the Middle Kingdom.
1991–1783?	Northern Nubia reconquered. War-like expeditions to Palestine.
1640?	End of the Middle Kingdom. Hyksos rulers from Palestine. Hyksos introduce horse-drawn war chariots and iron working.
1550?	Egypt re-united as Hyksos driven out. Capital at Thebes. Northern Nubia and parts of Palestine reconquered.
1504–1492?	Thotmes I creates Egyptian Empire by conquering more of Nubia, Palestine, and Syria.
1473–1458?	Hatshepsut becomes queen with as much power as the pharaohs.

1391–1353	Under Amenhotep III, the Egyptian Empire is at its peak.
1353–1335?	Akhnaton builds new capital at Akhtaton, and forces Egyptians to worship only the Sun god Aton. Art develops a new style.
1333–1323?	Rule of Tutankhamen. Capital moved to Memphis. The old religions brought back.
1307–1070?	Pharaohs called Ramses build great monuments. Egypt loses control of Palestine and Nubia.
1070?	End of the New Kingdom. Priests of Thebes begin ruling Upper Egypt.
770?	Nubians conquer most of Upper Egypt.
712	Nubians conquer the rest of Egypt.
664	Necho I drives out Nubians and makes Egypt independent.
525	The Persians conquer Egypt.
332	Alexander the Great of Greece conquers Egypt. The city of Alexandria is built.
30	Egypt becomes a province of the Roman Empire.

AD

394	Egypt becomes almost completely Christian.
640	Arabs conquer Egypt. Egyptians convert to Islam.

GLOSSARY

absolute ruler king whose power to govern is not limited by law

akhet season of the Nile flood, August to October

anatomy study of bodies, often human

archaeologist person who tries to work out what happened in the past by finding and studying old buildings and objects

astronomy study of the movement and position of the stars

ba part of a person's soul that the Egyptians believed could travel to the underworld

cataract large waterfall that prevented boats from passing

civilization large group of people who have settled in one place and live in the same organized way

delta fan-shaped area of muddy land at the place where a river divides and flows into the sea

demotic script simplified form of the ancient Egyptian hieratic script, used between 700 BC and 450 AD

dynasty line of rulers belonging to the same family

early period the time of the first and second Egyptian dynasties (3100–2694(?) BC)

excavate carefully dig up buried objects to find information about the past

Greek period the time following Alexander the Great's conquest, when the pharaohs spoke Greek and Alexandria became the main centre of Greek civilization (332–30 BC)

hieratic script simplified form of Egyptian writing that first appeared during the early period

hieroglyphics Greek word for an elaborate form of Egyptian writing, used for formal messages such as inscriptions, that used both pictures and sound signs

hunter-gatherers people who live by hunting for animals, and gathering plants for food

Hyksos people who invaded Egypt from Palestine, and ruled Egypt during the 15th and 16th dynasties

inscription formal message set down in a long-lasting form, such as being carved in stone

irrigation system of watering crops by channelling water from a river along pipes or ditches

ka body-spirit that the Egyptians believed could not survive unless the dead person's body was mummified

Lower Egypt part of Egypt that included the Nile Delta and the Nile Valley as far south as Memphis

Middle Kingdom the second great age in Egypt (2040–1640(?) BC)

New Kingdom the last great age in Egypt (1550–1070(?) BC), including the last days of the Egyptian Empire

nomarch Greek word for the governor of a nome, which was a small Egyptian province

Old Kingdom the first great age in Egypt (2649–2134(?) BC), when most of the pyramids were built

papyrus reed that grew in Nile swamps; the shoots were a luxury food, the stems were woven together to make boats. Papyrus sheets were used for writing on.

peret season of planting and fresh growth, from November to February

pre-dynastic period the time before Egyptian history began

regent someone who rules on behalf of a child who is too young to come to the throne

sacrifice thing or person that is given up (or killed), often as an offering to a god

shemu dry season from March to August, when crops ripened and were harvested

shrine holy place where believers keep an object that they link closely with a god or spirit

step pyramid tomb or temple built up of layers, each layer being smaller than the one below

true pyramid tomb or pyramid with a square base and four outside walls in the form of triangles that meet at the top

underworld world of the afterlife, where the Egyptians believed that the Sun god came back to life each night

Upper Egypt part of Egypt that included the Nile Valley from Memphis, south to the first cataract

vizier Arabic word for the scribe who was the chief adviser to the pharaoh

Further reading

You can find out more about the Ancient Egyptians in books and on the Internet. Use a search engine such as www.yahooligans.com to search for information. A search for the words "Ancient Egypt" will bring back lots of results, but it may be difficult to find the information you want. Try refining your search to look for some of the people and ideas mentioned in this book, such as "Osiris" or "pyramids at Giza."

More Books to Read

Encyclopedia of Ancient Egypt (Usborne Publishing, 2004)

The Egyptians, Rachel Wright, Nicola Baxter (Franklin Watts, 2001)

The Great Pyramid (Ticktock Media Ltd, 2005)

INDEX